W9-BSW-646

essential careers™

A CAREER IN
CUSTOMER SERVICE
AND TECH SUPPORT

JEFF MAPUA

ROSEN
PUBLISHING®

NEW YORK

Published in 2015 by The Rosen Publishing Group, Inc.
29 East 21st Street, New York, NY 10010

Library of Congress Cataloging-in-Publication Data

Mapua, Jeff.
A career in customer service and tech support/Jeff Mapua.—First Edition.
        pages cm.—(Essential careers)
Audience: Grades 7 to 12.
Includes bibliographical references and index.
ISBN 978-1-4777-7886-9 (library bound)
1. Customer services—Vocational guidance—Juvenile literature. 2. Computer technical support—Vocational guidance—Juvenile literature. I. Title.
HF5415.5.M165 2014
658.8'12023—dc23

                                                                              2014007270

Manufactured in the United States of America

contents

INTRO

A career in customer service and tech support may appeal to anyone who loves to help people and solve problems.

DUCTION

It's Ruby's birthday, and she received a computer. She's excited about using it, but there seems to be a problem. Ruby's not a technical person, so she can't figure it out on her own. The manual does not have all the answers she is looking for, and Ruby's family is stumped. Who does she ask for help?

Luckily for Ruby, the computer company offers customer support to everyone who purchases its products. All Ruby has to do now is call the number for the company's help line and talk to one of the representatives. If Ruby gets the service she needs, the company may win over a customer and more of her future business.

Customer service representatives are on the front lines of a company's interactions with consumers or people who buy products. They are there to answer questions like: What is the status of my order? Or, my product seems to be missing a part, what can I do? Technical support representatives work in a similar way. However, tech support helps customers who may not have the ability to address a complicated technology problem. Both customer service and tech support representatives interact with consumers on a daily basis. This is especially true for large companies with millions of customers.

Because of the reliance of customer support by any company providing a product or service to consumers, there will always be a need for representatives. No product is perfect, and customers will have questions. These questions can range from simple to important problems that expose flaws. Customer service representatives have traditionally completed most of their work in person or on the phone, but more recently, they help customers online through chat applications on a computer.

Technical support specialists resolve problems by troubleshooting, or finding and eliminating problems, and problem solving. Successful technical support specialists use a combination of experience, knowledge, and creativity to help customers find their solutions. Like customer service representatives, tech support can be done in person, over the phone, or even on the computer—as long as the problem is not the computer itself, of course.

Unlike other careers that are dependent on a healthy economy, such as luxury services, the customer service and technical support industries are more stable. The Bureau of Labor Statistics, a fact-finding agency for the U.S. government, predicts that the number of customer service representative jobs will grow 15.5 percent between 2010 and 2020. This means that there will be approximately 338,400 more jobs available within that time period. Customer service and tech support representatives need to possess not only a knowledge of their company's products and industries, but they must also have great people and communication skills. It is a challenge to balance professionalism with technical skills, but those who accomplish this feat find it very rewarding.

chapter 1

THE BUSINESS OF CUSTOMER SERVICE AND TECHNICAL SUPPORT

When choosing a career, there are many factors to consider. Things like average salary, stability within the industry, and your personal interests are key to finding something both satisfying and financially stable. One thing you should consider is how many companies employ people for your chosen job. For example, while one company may rely heavily on video editors, another company may have no use for them. Some occupations are important to a large number of companies and would therefore be a great career to pursue.

Jobs in the technical support or customer service industries are examples of jobs that are important to a large number of companies. As most companies now have some kind of interaction with customers and use technology for their daily operations, industries of all kinds, from financial institutions to aerospace manufacturing to book publishing, need great customer service and technical support.

WHAT IS CUSTOMER SERVICE?

The main role of a customer service representative is to connect a business with its customers. While many employees at a company work away from public view, customer service interacts directly with people who purchase the company's products or use its services. Representatives find solutions to difficulties a consumer might have with a product or service. If the representative cannot find a solution, he or she can refer the consumer to an expert who can. Due to the nature of the occupation, many customer service representatives must be patient, diplomatic, and able to sympathetically deal with people. People who call a business to fix a problem with their product may be feeling frustrated or angry. For example, if a customer orders a product and an incorrect one is sent instead, that customer may become upset. Customer service representatives must be tactful, respectful, and understanding in order to resolve the problem without insulting or further frustrating the consumer. A frustrated customer is unlikely to return for more business.

WHAT IS TECHNICAL SUPPORT?

Technical support has really only been around for a few decades. However, the technology industry has grown at a very high rate as more people buy products like smartphones, computers, and other electronics. There are companies that sell high-tech solutions to other businesses, too. As the number of these companies increase, so does the tech support industry.

Like customer service representatives, tech support specialists interact with consumers daily to help resolve their

Patience and sympathy are important qualities in a good customer service representative when interacting with frustrated clients.

questions and problems. Tech support specialists must be knowledgeable about their company's products in addition to technology in general. Communication is very important. One customer may know everything about computers while another may have a hard time with basic tasks. A technical support specialist must be able to communicate with both of them. This means he or she will have to speak in

YOUTH WORK ETHIC

A strong work ethic is important to all occupations. Work ethic is a person's set of values based on hard work and persistence. A person with a strong work ethic believes in being reliable, taking initiative, and practicing good social skills as the building blocks of great character.

Interestingly, different age groups place different values on work ethic. It is a common opinion among older generations that younger generations are not as hard-working as they were at their age. Research supports this claim and shows that work ethic is valued higher by older adults than younger adults.

A national survey showed that millennials, people born in the early 1980s to the early 2000s, do not consider work ethic as a defining quality of people their age. Further, work ethic was shown to be a quality that separates millennials from older generations such as baby boomers, or people born between 1946 and 1964. People of all age groups identify older generations as having a stronger work ethic in general.

With the economy hitting a low point in the early twenty-first century, work ethic is now more important than before. Many millennials are returning home after graduating college due to poor job prospects. In 2010, 37 percent of eighteen- to twenty-nine-year-olds were unemployed—the highest percentage in three decades. For those lucky enough to be employed, a strong work ethic may mean the difference between success and unemployment.

plain terms to a customer who does not know much about technology and use correct industry terms with a customer who does. Strong analytical skills are also important so that support personnel can problem-solve quickly.

WHAT DOES THE JOB ENTAIL?

Customer service and technical support personnel share many similarities. Both interact with numerous people daily, and resolve the product or service problems for customers or other employees. However, within those duties, there are several differences.

CUSTOMER SERVICE

The exact duties and responsibilities of a customer service representative will vary from company to company. Where one employer may require representatives to keep track of the number of calls, other employers may have an automated system

Technical support employees must be knowledgeable about the products their company sells in order to answer any question a customer may have.

that keeps track of calls with a computer program. Other customer service departments work mainly by phone, while others can work in-person or over the Internet.

However, there are some common duties among most customer service positions. Representatives are required to listen and respond to the needs and problems of customers. They provide information about their company's products and services. Whenever a consumer has a return or a complaint, it is up to the customer service department to address the issue. A customer service department's duties include resolving any problems brought by consumers. A discovery process may require communication with supervisors, managers, or other departments that have the necessary answers.

Customer service is also responsible for taking orders from customers, determining the final price and fees required for orders, and managing billing and payments. Some companies keep records or accounts of their customers, and customer service representatives are responsible for maintaining these records. This includes recording the details and history of a customer's interactions with a company.

Most customer service departments operate out of telephone call centers. Representatives may focus on a particular form of communication, such as phone calls, Internet chats, or e-mail. It is common for customer service to communicate by more than one method. Once a customer contacts a company, the representative then accesses that particular customer's records and files using the business's customer history system. Following the company's guidelines, the customer service representative finds a solution to the customer's issue. If the representative cannot find a solution, then a coworker or supervisor may provide additional help. Once the problem is resolved, the status of the call is recorded and the representative moves on to the next customer.

In addition to normal duties, customer service representatives may be required to help improve a company's call center. This could include projects such as maintaining the customer records database or coming up with improvements to the overall help process.

TECHNICAL SUPPORT

There are different types of technical support. One type assists customers or people who use a service provided by a company. Another type of technical support assists other employees within a business with various technology problems. For example, when an employee has an issue with a work computer, the tech support representative or help desk technician finds a solution. Technical support can also assist a sales team's presentations to potential customers. While a salesperson can describe the benefits of a product, the tech support representative is there to answer specific questions about the technology.

Because there are so many different types of technical support, there are a large number of skills involved. Not all technical support positions require employees to be experts at all technology skills, but many require some level of technological knowledge.

Specialists who assist other employees are responsible for their company's networks, as well as analyzing, troubleshooting, and evaluating problems. The internal information technology, or IT support team tests and evaluates a company's network system and performs regular maintenance of systems and hardware. Most communication is conducted by phone or e-mail, although within a company, some problems can be addressed in person. It is important for a company's internal technology problems to be solved quickly. Organizations depend on technology running properly to conduct business. It is a major problem if a system such as a company's e-mail service fails.

Technical support employees who interact with customers typically respond via phone calls and e-mail. In more difficult

There are different types of technical support opportunities in several industries.

cases, tech support will go to a consumer to solve problems in person. Tech support diagnoses or determines the source of a customer's problem. Once the problem is diagnosed, support can fix the problem and even teach the customer what to do to avoid future problems. This includes training customers on

hardware or software, installation processes, and other technology-related tasks.

Sales tech support joins a salesperson on visits to potential customers. They assist with installations of their company's products onto a customer's system, and answer questions that come up during a sales presentation. Any issues that arise are then communicated back to their technology teams and management to help improve the product.

WHERE DO THEY FIT IN?

There are many different ways an organization may maintain its customer service and technical support staff. However, there are several common ways these departments are structured.

CUSTOMER SERVICE

Many customer service departments are based in call centers. The centers have enough phone lines for every employee to have his or her own dedicated line. Other organizations have their customer service departments in their own offices. Retail customer service employees often walk around stores to interact with customers as they browse for and purchase products. A small number of customer service representatives work from their homes. This is a newer concept, but is slowly gaining acceptance in the industry.

TECHNICAL SUPPORT

Most information technology teams work as their own separate departments, although those who work with salespeople may be part of the sales department. Technical support teams can sometimes work under network and computer systems administrators. These administrators handle more complex tasks while the technical support team handles the more common technical problems.

Due to the importance of keeping an organization's internal networks working correctly, most IT departments are located at a company's headquarters. Tech support teams that work directly with customers are usually located at their own call centers similar to customer service representatives. Since their duties are similar, technical support and customer service for a single company may be located in the same office. Other tech support specialists work from home. This is more common with sales-related tech support.

chapter 2

STARTING OUT

What skills does someone need to begin a career in customer service and tech support, and to be successful in those fields? There are a great number of classes offered by high schools. Taking the right courses are a good start should someone decide to get into the customer service and tech support industry.

WHAT ARE THE SKILLS NEEDED?

Employees in all careers need to be hard-working, responsible, and responsive to the needs of the company they work for. However, there are specialized skills needed to excel in customer service and technical support.

CUSTOMER SERVICE

According to a director at an organization specializing in improving customer service departments for other businesses, customer service is about building relationships. This means companies hire people who have strong communication skills, are good listeners, can solve problems quickly, and understand the work environment. Additionally, because there are so many different types of businesses with their own types of customer service, it is best to understand the industry of any company where you might like to work.

Customer service:
Good morning, how may I help you today?

Customer: I bought a toy for my son two weeks ago but it hasn't arrived yet!

Customer service: I'm so sorry for the inconvenience. Do you have your order number? I'll look that up for you and see what we can do to get that toy to you right away.

New innovations in technology create different ways companies can interact with the general public. Instant messaging is just one way businesses communicate.

Communication skills mean being able to listen well, speak clearly, and convey information accurately. Resolving a customer's problems begins with listening carefully and understanding what the person needs. After discovering the solution, customer service representatives must then be able to relay relevant information to the customer.

Because there are many different methods of communication, successful customer service means being able to interact with customers in person, through e-mail, and online chats, or on the phone. Written communication requires excellent grammar, spelling, and punctuation. All customer service representatives must maintain a friendly and professional attitude.

Customer service interacts with a high number of people on a daily basis. Therefore interpersonal skills are a vital part of successful customer service. These skills mean good communication, but they also mean having the ability to reduce the level of stress in a situation, resolving conflict, and managing anger. This can lead to greater familiarity, understanding, and confidence between a customer and a representative.

Creating a relationship with a stranger is one thing, but creating a relationship with a stranger who may be upset or angry is another situation altogether. Customer service fields phone calls and other types of communication from people who have a question or issue with a business's product or service. They may be in a bad mood, and customer service representatives must be able to speak to this person without losing their own temper. Remaining polite requires a critical skill—patience.

Finally, customer service representatives must have strong problem-solving skills. Every day customers will call, but rarely will the calls be the same. Solving each problem requires the

People expect technical support representatives to have strong troubleshooting and problem-solving skills.

ability to analyze the situation, discover the cause of the problem, and finding a solution. Putting all of these skills together will help a representative better understand the work environment and learn what it takes to be successful.

TECHNICAL SUPPORT

Technical support specialists must have a technological background with experience in various forms of technology. Customers expect technical support representatives to be more knowledgeable about computers and other types of

technology than they are—or at least more knowledgeable about the product that they are calling about.

Tech support speaks to a large number of people on a daily basis. Listening is a very important skill for tech support staff. Not only will specialists need to listen to coworkers and managers, they will also need to listen carefully to customers as they describe their problems. No matter if they work with customers or other employees, tech support must be able to quickly understand the problems that are presented.

Technical support staff must then be able to communicate solutions to other employees or customers. Technical communication can be seen as a form of translation from one language to another. Often, customers who have technology problems will not be able to understand the highly technical language of the industry. Tech support must be able to communicate with nontechnical people every day.

Communication skills also include writing. Since communication through e-mail and Internet chats is more common as technology is adopted in more businesses, writing skills are gaining importance. Writing skills also applies to creating instructions on how to complete various technical tasks. These instructions must be clear and easy to read.

Sometimes the solution to a problem is obvious to a tech support person, but not to the customer calling for help. Most people with any level of experience with computer software or hardware are aware of how frustrating it can be. In these instances, tech support must have strong interpersonal skills. This means being patient and understanding of the customer's frustration.

Problem-solving skills are also a requirement. Tech support must be able to troubleshoot, or systematically find the source of a problem. Customers will have both simple and complex issues with their products. It will be up to the tech support specialist to use logic, analyze problems, and then provide the correct solution.

SATS AND ACTS

Colleges and universities require applicants to take either the SAT or ACT. The scores from these tests are taken into consideration when a school decides to accept that person or not. Although either test may be enough for applicants, they are different from each other in significant ways. It will be to the applicant's benefit to learn which test may give him or her the best chance to get into college.

The vocabulary of these two tests is different. The SAT tends to have a stronger emphasis on vocabulary, while the ACT's questions are generally easier to understand at first glance. Those with a strong vocabulary may prefer the SAT.

While the SAT does not have a science section, the ACT does. The ACT's science questions are more about reading and reasoning skills rather than recalling facts. However, the ACT tests more advanced math subjects such as algebra I, algebra II, geometry, and trigonometry. The math questions are more direct than the SAT and do not try to trick the student.

Both tests have a writing section, although the ACT's writing section is optional. The SAT includes the essay in the final score, while the ACT keeps the writing score separate. Some schools, however, require a writing score from the ACT, so applicants must check to see if the writing portion is necessary for their school of choice.

The SAT test is broken up into smaller sections, and each section score is taken into account by admissions officers. The ACT, on the other hand, is more of an integrated or combined test, and the final score is most important to admissions officers. Both tests have their own quirks. Students are free to take both tests, but it is beneficial to understand what each offers.

HIGH SCHOOL COURSES

A high school diploma is the minimum requirement for either a customer service or technical support position. There are several high school courses that will help a career in either field.

CUSTOMER SERVICE

There are not many high school classes that are directly related to customer service careers. Instead, attaining overall skills is a good way to start. Students should take courses in math, business, computing, and English. Speech and communication courses can also be helpful for a career in customer service.

High schools offer business-related courses, too. Typing classes are useful for office-type jobs. Learning about common computer applications, such as word processing and spreadsheets, is also a good way to improve one's overall skills. Business management electives can help get an understanding of how businesses operate.

Students can begin developing their career skills in middle school and high school.

TECHNICAL SUPPORT

Getting the basics of technology is the first step in pursuing a career in not only tech support but all tech fields. Classes that teach computer science, the foundations of engineering, and electronics are great for anyone interested in a career in technical support. Some high schools offer helpful courses in schematic drawing, or drawing diagrams of mechanical or electrical systems using graphic symbols.

Math classes are vital to a technical support employee. Computer programming has much in common with mathematics and the logic it teaches. Math and science classes help develop analytical and critical thinking skills. English, speech, and other communication classes are very useful, too.

Students can look into a vocational high school that offers specific training in technology. Vocational schools may also be at the post–high school level. After high school, more intense training and education is available to college and university students. There are several types of degrees and certifications that are useful for someone in the tech industry. It is important to do research to find out what would be the most useful for your chosen field.

chapter 3

A Major Decision

What is the level of education and training needed for a job in technical support or customer service? The current economy puts employers in power when hiring for an open position. With so many applicants for a small number of jobs, a company can ask for more out of candidates. This means that employers may require a college degree for most positions. Finding a job is very competitive, and those with the appropriate level of education and most applicable skills have the best chance of getting hired. Selecting a major and choosing the right courses to take is an important step in beginning any career.

Applicable Majors

An associate's or bachelor's degree is necessary for most occupations. An associate's degree usually takes two years to complete, while a bachelor's degree generally takes four years. While most positions require a bachelor's degree, some companies may accept an associate's degree. Associate's degrees may also include on-the-job training. This hands-on experience can be as beneficial as a four-year degree. Students should think carefully about what they want from their careers before choosing a degree program. For some, it might be better to have hands-on experience. For others, having the bachelor's degree might ensure a job right out of school. Then there is the time factor

Colleges and universities offer classes that help students attain abilities that companies desire in their employees.

involved. Students should think about how soon they would like to enter the workforce.

A bachelor's degree is earned for completing a college education. A major, on the other hand, is the specific set of courses or area of study a student pursues at a college or university. For example, a student can major in mathematics, and after completing the requirements will earn a bachelor's degree in mathematics. Next, we will look at the best majors for students interested in customer service or technical support.

CUSTOMER SERVICE

Some colleges offer an associate's degree in customer service. The degree prepares students by teaching the fundamentals of customer service and the framework or makeup of the industry. It is common for the coursework for an associate's degree in customer service to include classes on customer relationship management, process standards, and the philosophy of customer service.

Customer service degrees are sometimes paired with courses and degrees for hospitality. The focus is on developing hospitality services and customer partnerships. Real-world scenarios are discussed with the intention to prepare students for a successful career. Classes teach students to communicate professionally with different levels of an organization either in written, oral, or visual forms. The newest trends and concepts are taught along with the industry standards.

Some schools teach specific customer service skills like learning how to work in call centers, at a help desk, and online. These classes show students how to properly address a customer's problem or question. Lessons focus on how to interact with customers on the phone or through e-mail. Technical training includes operating computer systems, data entry, and database and Internet use.

Some colleges offer four-year degrees in customer service or customer service management. One school's degree in customer service is designed to prepare students to interact with customers and business representatives. Other classes teach consumer issues, supervising a team, how workplaces differ, and professional development. There are many related majors that apply to the customer service industry. These majors include business administration, e-commerce, management, marketing, and public relations.

TECHNICAL SUPPORT

The technology industry moves very fast, and it is difficult for many schools to keep up with the latest innovations and trends. New courses and fields of study are introduced every year, so students are advised to check with their schools to determine what works best for them.

Many classes give students an opportunity for hands-on training in their chosen careers.

Some lower-level positions do not require a bachelor's degree, but they do require at least a solid knowledge of computers and systems. Still, most employers prefer to hire people with a bachelor's degree. Popular majors among tech jobs are computer science, computer engineering, information science, and information technology. Some schools offer computer support specialist degrees as well. The content of most of these degrees are different, but all help increase problem-solving skills and technical knowledge.

Computer science majors are required to take many programming courses. There are a large number of programming languages, such as C++ and Java. Pursuing a degree in computer science will include many hours debugging programs while working on a computer. The goal is to learn about computers, how people interact with them, and the design theory of software.

Information technology degrees are a combination of technology skills, business, and communication. Classes teach students how technology fits into a business and how computers support systems like communication and research. Students will not only gain knowledge about computer hardware and how people interact with them, but also strong technical and communication skills.

Computer engineering students learn about how computers work and how they can be improved. Classes may include seemingly unrelated classes such as physics or other sciences, but through those classes, computer engineering majors learn about designing and developing computer hardware and software.

COLLEGE COURSES TO TAKE

There are different course requirements and philosophies at every school. The required and elective classes a student takes for the same degree can be very different.

CUSTOMER SERVICE

Before taking classes toward a degree, some schools have prerequisites or classes a student must complete first. These classes may include English, public speaking, and basic computing to teach the fundamentals of common software and technology.

VOCATIONAL SCHOOLS

Vocational schools are commonly known as trade, career, or correspondence schools. Rather than teaching a general area of study as at a college or university, vocational schools teach specific skills and train for a job. After graduation, some schools help their students apply for jobs by identifying potential employers.

Some students may find benefit in the training offered by a vocational school, while others may find that employers provide all the training they need. Vocational schools often offer certification in a chosen field. Others allow their class credit to be transferred to a college or university. The lower cost of a vocational school as compared to a two- or four-year college degree could also be a better option for students.

However, some vocational schools are not as reputable and fail to teach the skills necessary for employment. Some schools have been known to exaggerate facts about the jobs they train for. For example, the average salary for a position may not match what the school advertises, or its training programs may not be as thorough as promised. Be sure to thoroughly research the reputation of any school you choose by asking other students or people responsible for hiring in the field, or by checking its rating on consumer advocacy sites such as the Better Business Bureau, which registers consumer complaints.

Students are also recommended to tour the school's facilities and research what equipment the school provides students, who the instructors are, total costs, and the program's success rate. The completion rate can reveal how current students feel about the program. A high dropout rate could mean students do not find the program helpful. Finally, students should find out if a school is accredited, or meets an official standard of education. Accredited schools can be found on the U.S. Department of Education's website.

There are similar prerequisites for a bachelor's degree in business administration, marketing, and other majors. Each school has different requirements.

Some schools offer courses that specifically teach customer service. These courses discuss how to develop a business philosophy focused on customers. They also examine the value of building a relationship with a customer. Current trends in customer service are debated with the goal of gaining an understanding of the strategies used by leaders in this industry. Then strategies, or best practices, are identified along with barriers to great customer service. Other courses focus on customer service management and how to properly run a customer service department.

Business-related courses can include business administration, accounting, management, marketing, public relations, and economics. These courses cover topics such as the American economy, business operation, and business techniques. They present the general background and business concepts of how to conduct yourself in a work environment.

Other courses emphasize customer interaction. Popular majors in this area are hospitality or human resources. Hospitality, or the friendly reception and entertainment of guests, is a central component of the lodging, food service,

Some college courses may provide call center training to prepare students for real-world jobs.

travel, tourism, and gaming industries. Human resources, or employee management, is a study of how people fit in an organization. Classes focus on the management of employees, staffing, training, and employee development. Human resources concentrates on creating a positive environment for a company's employees.

E-commerce classes teach students about doing business online, while various management classes discuss successful methods of handling a company's product supply. Related electives, or classes chosen by the student, can include anything from education and communication to political science and psychology.

TECHNICAL SUPPORT

Technical support employees generally have degrees related to technology. Prerequisites may include completion of advanced math classes, a science course, and basic computing knowledge. Common among the technology degrees are classes like calculus, discrete mathematics, logic, and other computer classes.

Technical support degrees are available from two-year and four-year colleges. Classes for these degrees include mathematics, logic, IT applications, database concepts, and IT customer service. A technical support degree trains students on how to evaluate hardware and software systems, interact with users, and provide support for a variety of work environments.

Computer science degree classes include computer system organization, data structures and algorithms, digital system design, mathematics, software engineering, and computer science. Students learn the theoretical foundations of computer science and apply them toward different topics of technology. The topics include animation, artificial intelligence, software engineering, and much more. Mathematics is also a vital part of a computer science degree.

A degree in information technology typically includes courses in programming, computer networking, computer systems and architecture, database management systems, computer science, and web technologies. These courses are designed to develop critical thinking skills. The major is often related to a business degree with graduates going on to jobs with business and technology companies.

Computer engineering courses include computer architecture, data structures, various programming languages, software systems design, and systems programming. Computer engineers design computer systems and make sure that they are reliable and available to the system's users. There is also a concentration on electrical circuits and networks. Computer engineering requires creativity when designing systems.

chapter 4

LOOKING FOR WORK

Graduation day has passed, and now it is time to take what you have learned into the workforce. Which types of businesses have customer service and tech support positions? What alternatives to full-time employment are there? Finally, are there things people can do to increase their attractiveness to potential employers?

THE HIRING TYPE

Full-time employment means dedicating a minimum of forty hours a week at a place of business. With that amount of dedicated time, it is important to choose a business in an interesting and personally engaging industry. Which businesses hire customer service and tech support positions?

CUSTOMER SERVICE

In 2010, the U.S. Census Bureau reported that there were approximately 2.2 million customer service jobs. Some of those positions were remote with people working from home while other employees worked in a call center. Industries that hired for customer service positions included insurance agencies, banks, and retail stores.

Most customer service representatives are not employed at companies with traditional products. Instead, these are companies

Job seekers who are prepared with the right training are in a better position to get hired.

that perform the customer service functions for other businesses. These companies are part of the administrative and support services industry.

A company may have a need for a customer service department. Rather than buy office supplies, hire staff, and train employees, the company can hire another company that already has the equipment and staff necessary to run a customer service team. The company trains the customer service representatives about their particular company. This particular industry is growing as more businesses choose to obtain work from an outside provider, or outsource, their routine support functions. The reason is because the administrative and support services companies specialize in certain business activities like customer support and carry them out more efficiently than most organizations.

Another industry that employs a large number of customer service jobs is retail. Businesses in this industry buy and sell goods and are the final step in the distribution of merchandise. The two main types of retailers are store and non-store. Non-store retailers include catalog, mail-order, and online shopping. As the final step in the distribution of merchandise, people in these jobs have a large amount of interaction with customers.

Companies in credit intermediation also employ a large portion of the customer service representatives in the United States. This industry is related to finance. Companies lend funds or issue credit through activities like mortgage and loan brokerage, check cashing services, and more.

Wholesale trade businesses hire many customer service representatives. Similar to the retail industry, wholesale trade companies are a step in the distribution of goods and services. Unlike retail, there is not as much interaction with the general public. Instead, wholesale trade businesses sell to other companies such as those in the retail industry. Customer service representatives working for wholesale businesses provide business-to-business support.

Insurance carriers employ many customer service representatives. These companies deal with selling and providing insurance to people and organizations. Many interact with the general public. A company that offers car insurance deals with a large number of customers. These customers may have questions about their insurance policies or need to file an insurance claim or a demand for reimbursement.

TECH SUPPORT

In 2010, there were about 607,100 tech, or computer, support specialists in the U.S. workforce. With greater consumer electronics available, some were able to work from home. Others worked in an office, while some even traveled to clients' locations. The most common industries that specialists worked in were information technology, education, finance, health care, and telecommunications.

According to the U.S. Census Bureau, the computer systems design and related services industry employed the largest number of tech support employees in 2010. Companies in this industry provide IT services. Activities include writing, modifying, testing, and supporting hardware and software for customers. They can also plan and design computer systems to work with other technologies. Other services include managing a client's computer systems and data processing facilities.

The educational services industry is another popular employer of tech support specialists. This industry includes schools, colleges, universities, and training centers of all kinds. Both public and private schools offer tech support positions. Positions at schools typically lend support and assistance to both faculty and staff members. Other positions may provide technical help to students, too. Any hardware or software issues a teacher, student, or department may have will be part of the tech support representative's responsibility. This includes lab equipment, printers, and computerized records and databases.

Companies that specialize in areas such as publishing, motion picture and sound recording, broadcasting, and telecommunications are part of what is known as the information industry. Many tech support representatives work for companies within this industry. They help produce and distribute books, movies, music, and more. Others provide a means to

Part of the hiring process for a technical support team may include being evaluated as you solve a real-world problem.

distribute these products by traditional methods or modern transmission, such as over the Internet. As technology grows, more companies involved with web searching and data processing are growing parts of the industry.

The U.S. Census Bureau lists the finance and insurance industry as a major employer of tech support services. These companies are responsible for financial transactions or facilitating such transactions. These include making loans, purchasing financial instruments like securities, selling and paying out insurance policies, and monetary control—which regulates the interest paid by depository institutions. These types of companies are more dependent on computers and technology than in the past. Ensuring that their systems are dependable is a major job duty for their technical support staffs.

GRADUATE SCHOOL?

After graduating college, many students are faced with a choice: Should they continue on in their education or join the workforce? Graduate schools offer an even higher level of education beyond a bachelor's degree. The decision has many factors that play a part. Many hope that graduate school will help them find better jobs. Is that really the case? Graduate school can be very expensive and will require a major commitment in time and effort. Are the benefits great enough to warrant the cost?

There are several key factors that students should understand before making a decision about graduate school. Experts say that students will not know if grad school is the best option for them until after being a part of the workforce. They say that it is rare that grad school is a good option immediately after completing a bachelor's degree. It is a mistake to enter graduate school without a career plan. Being unable to find work is not reason enough to commit to grad school.

Some students choose graduate school so that they can work as a professor in their field, but finding work is just as difficult, if not more so, in the academic world. The employment opportunities in academia are not as strong as they were in the past. There is no guarantee that a graduate degree will lead to a teaching position.

Students should ask themselves several questions before making a final decision, such as: What kind of financial support will they need? How many courses are graduate students required to take? How many years does it normally take to graduate? What type of employment opportunities are graduate students able to find after school? If the answers to these questions still point to attending graduate school, then students should make the commitment at a reputable school.

APPRENTICESHIPS AND INTERNSHIPS

An option for those looking to begin a career in either customer service or tech support is to find an apprenticeship or an internship. An apprenticeship functions to train new employees and provide them with on-the-job experience. Apprentices' wages increase as they become more skilled and learn about their chosen careers. Most apprenticeships last four years and end with a recognized credential that is useful for advancing a career.

An internship, on the other hand, is usually a non-paid position within a company. Although interns earn no pay for their time, internships can be great gateways into a stable career. The number of internships has increased sharply since they were mostly limited to the medical field in the 1950s. Unfortunately, many companies take advantage of interns and do not give them opportunities that were given in the past.

An apprenticeship or internship provides real-world experience that can give a potential employer more reason to hire a candidate.

CERTIFICATIONS AND LICENSES

Some jobs require certifications or licenses as proof of ability. Some employers will provide training so that employees can earn a certificate or license. Certifications and licenses are also a good way to improve one's chances at getting hired, sometimes even for jobs that don't require one.

Many organizations offer certification and license programs. Some are more recognized than others, so students must research each to find one that suits them best. Customer service representatives for insurance or financial services usually require a state license.

There are a large number of technology-related certifications available. Certifications are specific to a piece of hardware or software. Some software programs are very common among all businesses, while others are rarer. Find out what kinds of certification programs you need before committing time to one.

chapter 5

GETTING HIRED

T he United States' economy has highs and lows over time. While one decade may find the economy booming and numerous jobs available, another decade may find the economy weak and employment hard to come by. Although there were signs of improvement in 2013, the United States entered 2014 still affected by a recession that began years earlier.

As a result, job seekers have had to sharpen their search methods and what they can bring to a potential job to make employers more interested. Those in the customer service and tech support industries are no different.

JOB SEEKING

The Internet is the job seeker's primary resource. However, relying only on an Internet job board is a poor strategy, according to job recruiters. These recruiters seek good candidates for open positions, and they suggest focusing the job search, using online resources wisely and developing a network of contacts.

Focusing the job search means deciding on the type of work they prefer, identifying the companies that fit their desire, and choosing a location where they are comfortable.

There are many websites that post job openings. Some are open to all industries, while others are specific to a particular field. Online discussion boards and forums are

Job seekers can request an informational interview with a person in the human resources department of a company they are interested in to learn more about the company.

helpful for researching the opinions of those currently working in the industry. Companies may post jobs only for members of an association. Becoming part of organizations within your field can increase the chances of finding the perfect job.

NETWORKING

Experienced job seekers have learned that the phrase "It's not what you know, it's who you know" can be true when finding work. This is because companies tend to favor someone they know or someone recommended by someone they know over an unknown person. For this reason, many employment advisors suggest creating a network of people or contacts.

Through these contacts, job seekers can learn about open positions before they are advertised on a website or job board. Some jobs are never even advertised, and only those with the right connections get an opportunity at landing the position.

Building a network requires meeting new people and learning about what they do. Industry-related events, such as a conference or expo, are a proven method to getting in touch with the right people. Joining an industry-specific organization can help you find connections, training classes, and seminars that will put you in touch with the right people.

Your network can be made up of anyone you know, including family, friends, and coworkers. Although it is helpful to have contacts within a preferred industry, there are many benefits to making connections with many other people. One friend may know of someone looking for a particular skill set. That friend can connect two people who have never met, and everyone benefits in the end.

Creating a network means communicating with other people and building a relationship. Although it is beneficial to meet a high number of contacts, career advisors suggest that network relationships should be meaningful. Contacts should share mutual career interests or friends. Through these relationships, job seekers can ask about specifics of the career.

However, don't ask about job openings too soon in a relationship. It is best to allow a friendship time to develop before asking about more sensitive topics related to the job market.

SALARIES

The salary for a customer service and tech support representative varies depending on the company. In 2011, U.S. News reported that the median annual salary for customer service representatives was $30,610. The highest salary was $49,800, while the lowest was $19,620. The best-paying industries were "industrial companies focused on oil and gas extraction, aerospace manufacturing, and energy-related parts manufacturing." Regarding salary by region, those living in San Jose, California; San Francisco, California; and Bridgeport, Connecticut, made the highest average salary. Since the early 2000s, the average salary for customer service representatives increased until the recession of 2008, when it began to decline, probably in response to the economy.

For computer support specialists, the Bureau of Labor Statistics found the average salary to be $46,260 per year, or $22.24 per hour. The lowest earned about $28,300, while the highest earned approximately $76,970. The highest concentrations of jobs were in tech-heavy job areas in Northern California and Seattle, Washington. Equipment manufacturing and software publishing industries paid more than the education industries. Since 2004, the average salary has increased by about $8,000. Many tech support positions offer full benefits, such as health care and paid vacation.

INTERVIEWING

The interview is the first time a potential employer will meet you. The employer hopes you are the one for the job. So it's important to be well prepared. Typically, an interviewer may ask, "Where do you see yourself in five years?" and "What is your greatest strength?" to find out what your

Salaries in the tech support and customer service industries can vary depending on company, location, and job title.

goals are and how you present your skills. However, some interview questions test thinking skills like, "Why are manhole covers round?"

For customer service representatives, U.S. News asked companies what questions they pose in interviews. One interviewer answered, "Tell me about a time when you had a difficult customer and how you handled it?" Another asks, "How do you define 'great customer service'?"

Tech support interviews tend to be more specific about the interviewee's technical skills and how they relate to a particular company. Questions may be similar to "Tell me about a time you helped a customer using your technical skills," or "How would you tell a friend how to install a printer?"

Some companies will also ask their job candidates to complete a test to show their skill levels. Hiring managers may also require interviewees to go through a practice customer call.

Always enter an interview prepared so that you can answer questions with confidence and ask your own questions to show your interest in the company.

UNDERSTANDING THE WORK ENVIRONMENT

Training and learning about the industry are great introductions to a career. However, actually experiencing day-to-day employment is the only way to get the career you want. What should someone expect to experience while working either in customer service or tech support?

CUSTOMER SERVICE

The needs of the industry drive the kind of support a customer service representative would need to give. Different personalities and unique company goals also make each customer service team different. However, many share several traits.

Most of a representative's day will be spent in front of a computer screen in a cubicle or small office. The phone will be in constant use. Many businesses supply their customer service teams with headsets to use with their phones.

Every business has its own process and equipment, but customer service representatives should expect to be issued a headset, phone, and computer.

For customer service teams working from a call center or office, it can get noisy with multiple people having simultaneous conversations. Sitting and typing all day can lead to physical problems, such as backaches and eyestrain. Health professionals recommend regular breaks to stretch and get the muscles moving. The work can be repetitive. Some find repetition comfortable, while others prefer more variety in their daily tasks.

As with most professions, customer service can be stressful. Many calls and interactions with the public begin with an agitated customer. Customer service representatives must be able to handle the challenge of angry callers, but also appreciate the polite and courteous interactions. It is also common practice for a business to keep track of its customer service team's work. This means that calls are recorded and statistics are kept about the number of customers helped. Some find the close supervision stressful, while others find it useful for self-improvement.

TECH SUPPORT

Generally speaking, tech support staff work in a comfortable business environment. Workweeks are forty hours long but can be longer depending on the workload or when technical problems arise, which may not be during normal business hours. As with customer service representatives, there is the possibility of working nights and weekends while in tech support. Some companies ask their employees to work holiday shifts, too.

Some companies may send their tech support employees to a customer's location to address whatever issue needs resolving. Additionally, tech support can travel with a member of their company's sales team to assist with answering tech-related questions, installing hardware or software, or presenting information to potential customers.

A position in tech support can be stressful for many of the same reasons customer service work can be stressful. Customers contact businesses about problems they encounter, and often they call while angry, upset, or confused. Communicating with someone with no technical background can be difficult, especially when the other person is in an agitated mood.

WORK SCHEDULES

Customer service and tech support teams are staffed with full-time and part-time employees. Full-time means working a minimum of forty hours a week, and part-time is anything less than that. Every company is different, and each has its own philosophy regarding work hours.

CUSTOMER SERVICE

According to the U.S. Census Bureau, most customer service employees work full-time, while about 20 percent work part-time. An organization may wish to have customer service available twenty-four hours a day. In these instances, customer service employees are assigned day or night shifts. There are different types of day shifts, including early morning or evening, while late-night shifts may extend into the early part of the day. Night shifts can be difficult to adjust to, and they often cause fatigue.

Additionally, it is common for a business to require weekend or holiday shifts. Retail stores adjust to the shopper's schedule, and this includes evenings, weekends, and holidays such as Thanksgiving and New Year's Day. Part-time positions can be available for seasonal work when consumers do the most shopping.

TECH SUPPORT

Most tech support specialists work full-time. Depending on the type of technical support, the department may be open during business hours or twenty-four hours a day. For example, if a company runs a website, its technical support staff will be available at all hours to ensure the site runs smoothly all day. In cases like these, tech support commonly works weekend, night, and late-night shifts.

There is a trend for businesses to hire their tech support on a contract basis. This means that a tech support representative is hired for a predetermined amount of time. At the end of the contracted duration, the representative could be rehired, released, or hired permanently.

chapter 6

MAKING A CAREER OF IT

After getting an education and training and finding a job in the industry, it may feel like time to rest and celebrate accomplishments. However, getting hired is just the first step on the path to a successful career.

UNDERSTANDING MANAGEMENT

There are aspects to customer service that can add stress to the job. While it may seem easier, from the perspective of the representative, to do away with these stressful job responsibilities, they provide a valuable service to the overall success of a company. For example, companies track each representative's work and number of customer contacts. These statistics are used to improve the overall quality of work, as well as ensure a minimum number of customers are helped each day. Although this puts pressure on the representative to quickly handle each call, improving each representative's abilities is part of the main goal.

Tech support specialists can have the same pressures as customer service. Both jobs may have supervisors listen to or record their calls for training purposes. For companies that have night shifts, new employees are generally expected to "pay their dues" and work the oddest hours. Those with longer tenures at a company are generally rewarded with more desirable shifts.

WORKING WITH OTHERS

Customer service and tech support employees typically work on a team or group. Business advisors suggest that all members of a team should understand the overall goals of the whole.

Customer service and tech support team members often work closely together.

Team members should be able to rely on one another for help and share knowledge and experience. Successful groups share interests and social and personal traits, and they cultivate a friendship. Communication, cohesiveness, sympathy, and collaboration are important to success.

WORKING WITH CUSTOMERS

Regardless of how customers may behave while speaking to a customer service or tech support representative, they deserve the support they are contractually entitled to. The level of help should be at least as good as the competitors and should leave a customer happy with the service. Help should be honest and professional.

Those with experience in the profession suggest the following steps to successfully help a customer. The first goal of the representative is to assure the customer that he or she will get help. This step is meant to keep focus on the customer, rather than on the needs of the representative. Second, employees must address the customers' requirements, or specifics to fulfill their needs. Representatives should repeat customers' requirements and explain what steps are necessary to meet them. Not all requirements are reasonable and can be met.

Next, the successful customer service and technical support representative will accommodate a customer's requests. This

A positive, memorable interaction with customer service can turn an occasional customer into a loyal one.

means finding time in the schedule to give an honest attempt at finding a solution. Some customers may have additional requests, such as communicating progress via e-mail. To find success, representatives should respect the customer's wishes.

Some customers may have their own suggestions, and best practices state that these should be respectfully considered. Obviously, not all suggestions will be helpful, but customers must feel like they are being respected. Finally, a representative sometimes must say no to certain wishes or requests. This means reshaping a customer's unrealistic demands. Specialists and representatives must avoid getting stuck and replying with a false statement or contradiction. It is best to specifically state what can be done and nothing more.

THE LATERAL MOVE

Not all career changes mean moving up or down in the business hierarchy. Career changes can be a lateral move, or a new job that keeps the job title, salary, or both from the previous job. Lateral moves can be the result of moving to a new city, changing industries, switching divisions within a company, or other similar changes.

There are benefits to choosing to switch to a position similar to one's current job. For example, another similar job may provide a chance for better advancement, or another position could be part of a growing team with good leadership. Lateral moves into a different industry can be a great career builder, too. Moving to a new company can lead to more contacts and a larger network. Additionally, new skills can be developed along with a deeper expertise.

Business advisors say that a fast upward leap in a career does not necessarily mean long-term success. A series of small upward steps mixed with lateral moves can lead to more success in the long run.

GETTING AHEAD

The key to advancement for customer service representatives is a comprehensive understanding of their company's product or service. Exhibiting the qualities of a good team member and having good people skills can lead to a promotion to a managerial or supervisory position. There is a possibility of even moving into the product development field for those with exceptional knowledge of their business.

Technical support specialists generally begin their careers focused on simple problems. Showing the ability to solve more complex problems can lead to higher pay or promotions. In addition to managerial or supervisory positions, promotions may lead to work in other areas of IT, such as systems administration or software development.

THE OUTLOOK

So what does the future hold? While no one can be certain, there are signs that both customer service and tech support industries are gaining strength despite the recent recession. Information about job growth for customer service industry positions is that they are growing on par with other occupations. Other research shows that firms continue to hire call center companies to outsource their customer service needs.

Technical support specialists may experience an even faster growth rate. From 2012 to 2022, the number of specialists is projected to grow 17 percent, faster than the average for all occupations. Companies will continue to upgrade their computer software and hardware and will need staff to maintain the new systems. New technologies will also affect the number of jobs, although the nature may change due to the type of technology such as cloud computing, where data is stored in another, centralized location.

There will always be businesses in need of good customer service and tech support to better assist their clients and buyers.

Ironically, technology may also negatively affect the job prospects for tech support and customer service departments. Internet self-service can reduce the number of jobs, and customers may be able to speak directly with employees directly involved with a product. This means representatives won't be needed to connect customers to specialists, but there will still be a need for customer guidance using the new technology.

Another threat to both industries is the practice of outsourcing. Since the early 2000s, the trend in business was to hire companies in other countries to run customer service and tech support departments. However, consumers have shown a preference for customer support based in the United States. Some organizations will continue to hire customer service and technical support teams in the the United States.

The job prospects for both customer service and technical support is good, according to Bureau of Labor Statistics. Customer service representatives who work for a business, as opposed to working in a call center that provides outsourcing, will find generally higher pay. This means more competition for these positions, but once in the company, there is better chance for advancement.

Technical support specialists will experience more favorable chances for advancement than most other positions. Those interested in a job in this industry will have a better chance for success with a bachelor's degree and a strong technical background. The information technology industry is expected to grow, and support services, making sure everything is working properly, will play a big part in a company's success.

Communication channels like social media, live chat, and other tools are expected to increase the amount of contact between a business and its customers. History and recent trends have shown that customer service and tech support are sturdy occupations and solid choices for a career.

glossary

accredited Granted official recognition and authorization.

aerospace An industry that deals with travel and vehicles for travel in air and space.

algorithm A process or set of rules to follow in problem-solving operations.

analytical Capable of examining in detail to understand meaning.

apprenticeship A system of training new employees by working for an expert in a trade.

cohesiveness The force bringing group members closer together.

consumer A person who purchases and uses goods or services.

contradiction A statement that is opposite of one already made.

diplomatic Skilled in handling sensitive or difficult situations.

elective A class chosen by the student.

hospitality The friendly reception of guests or strangers.

industry Trade or manufacturing enterprises in a particular field.

initiative Readiness and ability to make decisions and start an action.

intermediation The act of negotiating between two people or groups.

internship A position within a company with a focus on on-the-job training.

lateral In a direction to either side, as opposed to up or down.

manufacturing Making goods by machine or hand.

network A group of interconnected people who exchange information, contacts, and experience.

outsource To hire work from abroad or outside of a company.

personnel The people who work for an organization.

prerequisite A course that students are required to successfully complete before taking a higher level course.

reimbursement The repayment of compensation for an expense.

representative A person who represents an entity, such as a business.

requirement Something needed or a necessary condition.

resolve Find an answer or solution to a problem.

simultaneous Occurring at the same time or instant.

stability The state of something that is not likely to change.

strategy A plan or series of actions with a specific end goal.

troubleshooting Repairing failed products using a logical, systematic search for the source of a problem.

for more information

Bureau of Labor and Statistics (BLS)
Postal Square Building, 2 Massachusetts Avenue NE
Washington, DC 20212-0001
Website: http://www.bls.gov/home.htm
The Bureau of Labor and Statistics provides information about
economic conditions and the labor market to the public.

College Board
45 Columbus Avenue
New York, NY 10023-6992
(212) 713-8000
Website: http://sat.collegeboard.org
The College Board is a nonprofit organization that owns and
publishes the SAT.

Customer Experience Professionals Association (CXPA)
401 Edgewater Place, Suite 600
Wakefield, MA 01880
(781) 876-8838
Website: http://www.cxpa.org
The CXPA is a global nonprofit organization that supports
professional development of customer service
professionals.

Customer Service Institute of Canada
722 Crystal Court, Suite #1
North Vancouver, BC V7R 2B5
Canada
Website: http://www.csicanada.ca
CSI Canada is a national nonprofit member association

dedicated to the advancement of an industry association for customer service professionals.

HDI
121 South Tejon, Suite 1100
Colorado Springs, CO 80903
(800) 248-5667
Website: http://www.thinkhdi.com
HDI is a global membership, training, and certification association for technical service and support professionals.

IEEE
(800) 701-IEEE (USA and Canada)
Website: http://www.ieee.org
IEEE is a worldwide professional association. It is dedicated to advancing technological innovation and excellence globally, with more than 430,000 members worldwide in 160 countries.

Information Technology Association of Canada (ITAC)
5090 Explorer Drive, Suite 801
Mississauga, ON L4W 4T9
Canada
(905) 602-8345
Website: http://itac.ca
The ITAC is a not-for-profit, membership-driven organization that promotes the contribution that digital technology can make to Canada's economic prosperity.

International Organization for Standardization
1, ch. De la Voie-Creuse
CP 56

CH-1211 Geneva 20
Switzerland
Website: http://www.iso.org
The ISO is the world's largest developer of voluntary international standards. These standards give specifications that
make industries of all kinds more efficient and effective, as
well as helping international trade.

U.S. Census Bureau
4600 Silver Hill Road
Washington, DC 20233
(301) 763-4636
Website: http://www.census.gov
The Census Bureau gathers statistical information about
industries, the nation's people, and the economy.

WEBSITES

Because of the changing nature of Internet links, Rosen
Publishing has developed an online list of websites related to
the subject of this book. This site is updated regularly. Please
use this link to access the list:

http://www.rosenlinks.com/ECAR/Serv

for further reading

Bacal, Robert. *Perfect Phrases for Customer Service.* New York, NY: McGraw-Hill, 2010.

Bacal, Robert. *Perfect Phrases for Customer Service: Hundreds of Ready-to-Use Phrases for Handling Any Customer Service Situation.* New York, NY: McGraw-Hill, 2011.

Blanchard, Kenneth, Sheldon Bowles, Rick Adamson, and Kate Borges. *Raving Fans: A Revolutionary Approach to Customer Service.* New York, NY: Random House, 2004.

Brown, Andrew. *Tech Support 101.* Seattle, WA: CreateSpace, 2013.

Doepke, Darrell. *The Part-Timer Primer: A Teen's Guide to Surviving the Hiring Process and Landing Your First Job.* Sammamish, WA: Timbrewolfe, 2012.

Ensaff, Najoud, and Anne Rooney. *Retail Careers.* Mankato, MN: Amicus, 2011.

Evenson, Renee. *Customer Service Training 101: Quick and Easy Techniques That Get Great Results Paperback.* New York, NY: AMACOM, 2010.

Ferguson Publishing. *Business* (Careers in Focus). New York, NY: Ferguson, 2010.

Ferguson Publishing. *Telecommunications* (Careers in Focus). New York, NY: Ferguson, 2009.

Fischer, James. *Earning Money: Jobs.* Broomall, PA: Mason Crest, 2011.

Fodor, Jodi. *The SAT Word Slam: Rhyme Your Way to a Better Vocabulary and Higher SAT and ACT Scores.* Avon, MA: Adams Media, 2009.

Gallagher, Richard S. *Customer Service Survival Kit: What to Say to Defuse Even the Worst Customer Situations.* New York, NY: Amacom, 2013.

Goodman, John A. *Strategic Customer Service: Managing the Customer Experience to Increase Positive Word of Mouth, Build Loyalty, and Maximize Profits.* New York, NY: AMACOM, 2009.

Gordon, Sherri Mabry. *Using Technology: A How-to Guide.* Berkeley Heights, NJ: Enslow, 2012.

Graham, Ian. *In the Workplace. Information and Communication Technology.* London, England: Evans, 2010.

Guillain, Charlotte. *Jobs If You Like Computers.* London, England: Raintree, 2013.

Haugen, David M., and Susan Musser. *The Millennial Generation.* Detroit, MI: Greenhaven, 2013.

Marsh, Carole. *Would You Hire This Person?: A Look at Getting Hired (or Not!) ... from the Point of View of Your (Possible!) Future Employer.* Peachtree City, GA: Gallopade International, 2012.

McClenathan, Mike. *PWN the SAT.* Seattle, WA: CreateSpace, 2011.

Pierce, Alan J. *Introduction to Technology.* New York, NY: Glencoe/McGraw-Hill, 2010.

Rankin, Kenrya. *Start It Up: The Complete Teen Business Guide to Turning Your Passions into Pay.* San Francisco, CA: Zest Books, 2011.

Reed, Christie, and Taylor K. Barton. *Winning by Working.* Vero Beach, FL: Rourke Educational Media, 2014.

Reeves, Diane Lindsey, Joe Rhatigan, and Kelly Gunzenhauser. *Career Ideas for Teens in Business, Management, & Administration.* New York, NY: Ferguson, 2012.

Staudacher, Carol, and Susan M. Freese. *Job Search.* Costa Mesa, CA: Saddleback Educational Publishing, 2012.

Vaynerchuk. Gary. *The Thank You Economy Hardcover.* New York, NY: HarperBusiness, 2011.

bibliography

Bernstein, Alan B. *Guide to Your Career.* New York, NY: Princeton Review, 2004.

Big Future. "Major: Information Technology." Retrieved December 2013 (https://bigfuture.collegeboard.org/majors/computer-information-sciences-information-technology).

Bureau of Labor Statistics. "Educational Services: NAICS 61." Retrieved January 2014 (http://www.bls.gov/iag/tgs/iag61.htm).

Bureau of Labor Statistics. "Finance and Insurance: NAICS 52." Retrieved January 2014 (http://www.bls.gov/iag/tgs/iag52.htm).

Bureau of Labor Statistics. "Focused Jobseeking: A Measured Approach to Looking for Work." Retrieved January 2014 (http://www.bls.gov/opub/ooq/2011/spring/art01.pdf).

Bureau of Labor Statistics. "Information: NAICS 51." Retrieved January 2014 (http://www.bls.gov/iag/tgs/iag51.htm).

Bureau of Labor Statistics. "Retail Trade: NAICS 44-45." Retrieved January 2014 (http://www.bls.gov/iag/tgs/iag44-45.htm).

Federal Trade Commission Consumer Information. "Choosing a Vocational School." Retrieved December 2013 (http://www.consumer.ftc.gov/articles/0241-choosing-vocational-school).

Ferguson Publishing. *Internet.* 3rd ed. New York, NY: Ferguson, 2006.

Harvard Business Review. *Harvard Business Review on Advancing Your Career.* Boston, MA: Harvard Business Review Press, 2011.

Ohio University. "Patton College of Education: Customer Service." Retrieved December 2013 (http://www.ohio .edu/majors/undergrad/cehs/hcs/cs.cfm).

Perlin, Ross. *Intern Nation: How to Earn Nothing and Learn Little in the Brave New Economy.* London, England: Verso, 2011.

Pew Research Center. "Millennials: Confident. Connected. Open to Change." Retrieved December 2013 (http:// www.pewsocialtrends.org/2010/02/24/millennials -confident-connected-open-to-change).

Princeton Review. "The SAT vs. the ACT." Retrieved December 2013 (http://www.princetonreview.com/sat -act.aspx).

Sanchez, Andres R. *Technical Support Essentials: Advice You Can Use to Succeed in Technical Support.* New York, NY: Apress, 2010.

U.S. Bureau of Labor Statistics. "Computer Support Specialists." Retrieved December 2013 (http://www .bls.gov).

U.S. Bureau of Labor Statistics. "Customer Service Representatives." Retrieved December 2013 (http://www.bls.gov).

U.S. Census Bureau. "Administrative and Support Services." Retrieved January 2014 (http://www.census .gov/econ/census02/naics/sector56/561.htm).

U.S. Census Bureau. "Computer Systems Design and Related Services." Retrieved January 2014 (http:// www.census.gov).

U.S. Department of Labor. "What Is Registered Apprenticeship?" Retrieved January 2014 (http:// www.doleta.gov/OA/apprenticeship.cfm).

USNews.com. "Best Business Jobs: Customer Service Representative." Retrieved December 2013. (http:// money.usnews.com/careers/best-jobs/customer-service -representative).

USNews.com. "Customer Service Representative: Reviews & Advice." Retrieved December 2013 (http://money .usnews.com/careers/best-jobs/customer-service -representative/reviews).

USNews.com. "IT Manager." Retrieved December 2013 (http://money.usnews.com/careers/best-jobs/it-manager).

USNews.com Education. "5 Things You Need to Know About Graduate School." Retrieved December 2013 (http://www.usnews.com/education/blogs/the-college -solution/2011/06/28/5-things-you-need-to-know-about -graduate-school).

index

ABOUT THE AUTHOR

Jeff Mapua is a graduate of the University of Texas at Austin. He spent years working in customer service and technology support roles. He has worked in publishing for over ten years, covering a wide range of topics that include education and technology. His work has appeared in magazines, in books, and on several websites. Mapua lives in Dallas, Texas.

PHOTO CREDITS

Cover, p. 1 (figure) Piotr Marcinski/Shutterstock.com; cover, p. 1 (background) Eimantas Buzas/Shutterstock.com; p. 4 Paul Bradbury/OJO Images/Getty Images; pp. 8–9 Picturenet/Blend Images/Getty Images; p. 11 © AP Images; pp. 14–15 Jetta Productions/Blend Images/Getty Images; p. 19 oculo/Shutterstock.com; p. 21 auremar/Shutterstock.com; pp. 24–25 Steve Debenport/E+/Getty Images; pp. 28–29 Intellistudies/Shuttertock.com; p. 31 Purestock/Thinkstock; pp. 34–35 Wavebreak Media Ltd./Thinkstock; p. 39 Robert Daly/Caiaimage/Getty Images; pp. 42–43 Blend Images - Jetta Productions/Dana Neely/Brand X Pictures/Getty Images; p. 45 Rob Lewine/Getty Images; p. 48 Alexander Raths/Shutterstock.com; p. 51 Andrey Popov/Shutterstock.com; pp. 52–53 Konstantin Chagin/Shutterstock.com; pp. 54–55 Goodluz/Shutterstock.com; pp. 60–61 urbancow/E+/Getty Images; p. 62 Juice Images/Cultura/Getty Images; p. 65 Brian Jackson/iStock/Thinkstock.

Designer: Matt Cauli; Editor: Tracey Baptiste;
Photo Researcher: Karen Huang